D0790437

# TONY EVANS
## SPEAKS OUT ON
# SEXUAL
# PURITY

# TONY EVANS
## SPEAKS OUT ON
# SEXUAL
# PURITY

**MOODY PRESS**

CHICAGO

Scripture quotations are taken from the *New American Standard Bible*®, © Copyright The Lockman Foundation 1960, 1962, 1963, 1968, 1971, 1972, 1973, 1975, 1977. Used by permission.

ISBN: 0-8024-2561-5

5 7 9 10 8 6 4

*Printed in the United States of America*

# SEXUAL PURITY

Some years ago I took my wife, Lois, to play tennis. I will never do that again.

I explained the game to her. "You get over there, and I am going to hit the ball to you." I threw the ball up and hit it. Well, I knew I was in trouble when I saw her standing there with one hand on her hip, holding the racket as if to say, "You don't expect me to hit that ball, do you?" I knew this was going to be a long day.

I hit the ball over the net again, and she just watched it. I told her she had to run to the ball and hit it. She said, "I am not going to get all sweaty out here running after a little ball. If you want me to hit the ball back, you hit the ball to me." I was getting a little evangelically ticked off at this point.

So I hit the ball right to her. She took a Hank Aaron swing at it. *Bam!* She hit the ball way over the fence, then looked at me and told me to go get it. I said, "Let's go home; you can't play tennis outside the lines."

If you want to enjoy the game of tennis, you can't just hit the ball whenever and wherever you feel like hitting the ball. You can't run only when you feel like running. That is not tennis. That is madness.

That little episode on the tennis court is a humorous illustration of a very serious truth: You can't enjoy sex the way God intended you to enjoy it if you refuse to stay within the lines He has drawn.

The fact is, society keeps trying to blur those lines or erase them altogether. If you want to know our society's values and attitudes on sex, love, and moral purity, just listen to its music.

I grew up with popular singing groups such as the Temptations, the Miracles, the Delphonics, and the Dells. The basic message of their songs was "I love you. You love me. I lost you. You lost me. Can we get together again? Maybe." Today, the music helping to shape our young people's moral attitudes goes by titles like "I Want to Sex You Up" and "Nothing but the Dog in Me."

Sex dominates our popular culture to a degree we've never seen before. Prime-time television and the movie industry would be lost if they couldn't exploit sex. Talk shows wouldn't have anything to talk about without sex.

Unrestricted sex is being touted as a shortcut to personal fulfillment and satisfaction. People have given up their virtue for sex, traded their families for it—and now they're getting sick and dying because of it.

But in case you don't know, let me state right up front that sex is a wonderful and beautiful gift of God designed for human fulfillment. Sex is God's idea. But Satan has taken this God-ordained activity and has done with it what he does best. He has counterfeited it and sold his cheap imitation as the real thing.

So men lose their virginity trying to validate their manhood. Women sacrifice their purity seeking for someone to love and accept them. We have bought Satan's lie that immediate sexual gratification, regardless of the long-term cost, ought to be the driving force in our lives.

But the price tag for this purchase is high indeed: high in medical costs for AIDS and sexually transmitted diseases (STDs); high in the guilt that sends people to professional counselors; high in the death rate as unwanted children are aborted on the altar of convenience; high in welfare costs as the government must dole out money to take care of children who don't have a pair of parents to watch over them; and high in the divorce rate.

Sex is like an atom. Reduce it to its base elements, and you've got a problem the size of Hiroshima. You end up with lots of destruction and fallout but no joy. Clearly, this misuse of sex under the direction of the evil one is decimating our society. Sex is God's idea, and, therefore, it is good. But like anything else that God makes, when people get their hands on it and redefine it according to their own agenda, what is good becomes destructive. What was created in heaven becomes a mixture from hell.

That is what has occurred in the area of human sexuality. There is no place you can go in Western civilization to run from it. All you have to do is get in your car and drive down the highway—the billboards will let you know that sex sells. Some people will tell you that this blatant openness about sex is good because Christianity has suppressed and denied sex for too long.

I beg to differ. God has no hesitancy in talking about sex. He does not run from it. He does not blush when He deals with it. His Word puts it on the line when it comes to telling the truth about sex, and that's what I want to do in this booklet.

## THE PURPOSE OF SEX

First of all, why did God create sex? The most obvious reason is for procreation. The sexual relationship between a husband and wife became the method instituted to expand God's image in history.

Remember, God does not give us children just so that we can have lookalikes. God gives us children so that His image can be transferred. Parents are to stamp the image of God on their children so that when those children leave home, God's image and presence have been expanded in history.

A deeper purpose for sex, however, is to inaugurate, or initiate, the covenant of marriage. In another booklet in this series entitled *Divorce and Remarriage,* I spent a lot of time showing why God considers marriage to be a covenant every bit as serious as any other covenant

He has made. I refer you to that booklet as a helpful background to this issue.

Whenever God makes a covenant, He inaugurates it in blood. For example, God made a covenant with Abraham, the sign of which was circumcision (Genesis 17:10–12). All of the males born in Israel were to come as young boys and have the foreskin of their sexual organ removed to signify that they were part of God's covenant people. They were to be unlike everybody else.

Why was circumcision chosen as the sign of the Abrahamic covenant, which would establish Israel as God's special people and through which Abraham would become the father of many nations? Because this covenant was fulfilled and expanded as Abraham and his male descendants produced children.

Therefore their sexual organs would bear the mark of the covenant as a special sign that they and the children they fathered were set apart to the Lord. The rite of circumcision involved blood, which was part of the covenant.

So it is in marriage. Look at Deuteronomy 22:13–15:

> If any man takes a wife and goes in to her and then turns against her, and charges her with shameful deeds and publicly defames her, and says, "I took this woman, but when I came near her, I did not find her a virgin," then the girl's father and her mother shall take and bring out the evidence of the girl's virginity to the elders of the city at the gate.

The evidence was the blood-stained sheet or whatever garment was on the bed on which the couple consummated their marriage on the wedding night. Read the following verses and you'll see that, if the parents could prove their daughter's virginity, she was acquitted and the husband was fined.

But if there was no blood, meaning the woman was not a virgin prior to her marriage, she could be put to death (v. 21), because the covenant of marriage was inaugurated by blood. This passage also shows how God feels about sexual purity. Sexual immorality in Israel could be punishable by death, as the remaining verses of Deuteronomy 22 reveal clearly.

## THE VALUE OF SEXUAL PURITY

To say that God puts a very high value on sexual purity is to understate the case. The reason people give sex away so easily is that they don't know how valuable sexual purity is in God's eyes. Stuff you think is cheap, you throw away. Stuff that is expensive, you hold on to.

Lois and I dated for about two years before we were married. When we first started dating, she looked at me and said, "Let's get the rule straight up front. I am giving myself to one man, and that is the man I marry. That's it. Before we get this relationship started, if you have any other ideas, you are not the man I want to marry."

I knew right then that Lois was the woman I wanted to marry, because she was telling me that she was too valuable to just throw away her purity. She understood the value God placed on her, and on my purity too, and that commitment on her part attracted me to her.

That was the attitude in Scripture. It was a proud thing for a woman to be able to produce the evidence of her virginity and say to her parents and to all Israel, "I kept myself a virgin for my husband." Today, in popular society virginity is a joke. If you are a virgin, you are laughed at and scorned and talked about "sho' as you born," as the old folk used to say.

Not so in God's economy. In His view, a commitment to chastity before marriage is an act of consecration. Then the act of marriage is another form of consecration. Every time a husband and wife engage in sexual intercourse, they are saying afresh to each other, "All of me belongs to all of you." The sexual act within marriage is a reconsecration to the covenant.

So in Scripture the so-called recreational aspect of sex is never separated from the covenantal environment of sex. Marriage is the only "safe sex" program God has. Anything else, and you are on your own.

## GOD'S STANDARD FOR SEX

When God created Adam and Eve as opposite yet complementary sexual beings with a natural attraction for each other, Adam's statements about Eve in Genesis 2:23 show he understood that they were created for each other. And when God joined that first pair in marriage, there was no hesitation and no shame in their union. Theirs was the first and only perfect marriage, because sin had not yet polluted everything.

When God creates something, it produces ecstasy and not guilt. With Adam and Eve there was no "I should not have been there. I should not have thought that. I should not have done that." Whenever God does something, people are going to feel good about it. They don't have to hide.

---

*Today we have the "Alpo crowd."*

---

Obviously Adam and Eve were virgins before their marriage, so they had no reason to feel shame. It's true they were also sinless at this point, but the entrance of sin did not change God's sexual standards. Men and women were still expected to be virgins before marriage.

There were no double standards such as we have today, where men in particular make excuses for their sin by saying things like, "Well, I'm a man, and you know how men are about sex." No. You don't set the standard; God does.

I'm really concerned about this because we are raising a generation of young men, and even boys, who are like my dog. When my dog wants to satisfy his sexual desires, he goes looking for a female dog. His standards aren't very high. All he is concerned about is that his partner is a female.

When he comes back home, my dog shows no particular concern about what he has done. He can eat and sleep as if nothing happened. Whether that female dog is now carrying his puppies is of no concern to him. All he knows is that his passion has been satisfied.

What we have today is what I call the "Alpo crowd," a generation of men whose sexual standards are no higher than my dog's. They could not care less about the consequences to the woman. And they are not about to take responsibility for any children they may father. So you and I pick up the tab for their irresponsibility out of our paychecks as we pay for the welfare generation.

That is what happens when people abandon God's ideal for sex. You wind up with a generation of unwanted and uncared-for children, women with no one to marry, and men who have badly misunderstood the meaning of masculinity. It seems to me that we ought to go back to the Creator of sex to get our information right!

But instead, the wrong folks are doing the teaching on this subject. We are getting our information on sex from the guys on the street and from Dr. Ruth, Oprah, Geraldo, and others on television. Let's let God teach us. Let's let the Maker of sex do the sex talking, since He is not ashamed to talk about it.

Another tragedy today is that if your kids are in public school, they are most likely going to get some bad information. Even if your school does not dispense condoms, the "safe sex" mentality still colors a lot of what is taught. I thank God that we are seeing a little bit of light here as secular leaders begin to realize that abstinence makes sense for a lot of reasons.

God's sexual standard outside of marriage is virginity, an extremely valuable gift from Him that you can give away only once and never get back again. Yes, there is forgiveness for sin, and a person who has fallen sexually can rededicate himself or herself to Christ. But immorality in any form does tremendous damage. We must fight for God's standard.

## A BIBLICAL VIEW OF SEX

The church at Corinth had sexual problems. The Corinthians lived in a sex-crazed city, a port city where ships from all over docked. Corinth was the New York, the Los Angeles of its day. It was a happening place, built to service all of this activity and all of the merchants and sailors who came around.

In fact, on a hill in Corinth sat the *Ico-Corinthus,* the temple of Aphrodite, the goddess of love. This temple was divided into two halves. On one side was a restaurant, where a person could go in and have dinner. That's why we read in 1 Corinthians 8 about the problem of meat offered to idols. Christians were having trouble deciding whether they should go to the restaurant and eat meat that had been offered to pagan idols. On the other side of the temple were rooms that housed one thousand "sacred" prostitutes, who engaged in sex with worshipers as part of their pagan rites. Christians were living in this sex-crazed world, and it had rubbed off on them.

In 1 Corinthians 5, we read of a man in the church having an affair with his stepmother. In 6:9–11, Paul reminds the Corinthians that some of them came out of really messed up sexual backgrounds. But they had been "washed" and "sanctified" (v. 11), and they needed to remember who they were.

But someone might say, "Everybody else is doing it." God's answer is, "Since when are you everybody else? Since when does the crowd dictate what you are supposed to do?" Paul goes into a discussion of the hedonistic, pleasure-driven lifestyle that the Corinthian believers saw every day and what they should do to be different.

I am not unaware that many Christians today struggle with sexual sin, from fornication and adultery to homosexuality and any number of other deviant sexual behaviors. We are all susceptible to it.

It all stems from the same root —our sinful flesh, nurtured by a secular worldview that causes us believers to be governed by what the culture says and not by who we are in Christ. We all face it. Nobody is exempt from it unless he or she is dead, because our culture has made sure that we cannot run from it.

Well, Paul has a word for us. He says in verse 12, "All things are lawful for me, but not all things are profitable. All things are lawful for me, but I will not be mastered by anything." What he is saying is that God has rules that govern how we use what we have been given.

Sex is a legitimate passion, given to us by God. So if you are struggling sexually, you don't pray that God will take away your sexual urges. You are then asking not to be human. What you pray is that you not be mastered by your legitimate and lawful sexual urges so that the expression of them becomes your obsession no matter what God's rules say. Sex is part of your God-given makeup, but it was never designed to be your master. However, that's what sex has become in our culture.

You see, freedom is never doing what you *want* to do. Freedom is doing what you *ought* to do. Suppose a man stands on top of a tall building and announces, "I want to be free from gravity. I am going to do my own thing. So let me serve notice on you, gravity. I am in charge now. I am free." He leaps off the building, and for a couple seconds he is free. But it doesn't take long for it to dawn on him that he is not as free as he thought. That is confirmed as they sweep him up off the pavement. Gravity was running the show all the time.

The sidelines in football are designed to contain the game. Suppose the halfback decides, "I don't feel like being tackled today. I am not into sidelines. I think I'll run up into the stands, out into the concession area, into the parking lot, come around to the other side, run back through the concession area, down the stands, back onto the field, and across the other team's goal line for a touchdown. After all, I'm free." That's not freedom. You can't have football without sidelines. And as I said at the beginning, you cannot enjoy sex the way God designed for sex to be enjoyed if you operate outside of His rules.

It's like a fire. Contained in the fireplace, a fire keeps everybody warm. Set the fire free, though, and the whole house burns. You don't want the fire in your house to be free. You want it contained so that it can generate warmth and not destruction.

Those folks in Corinth were misguided about sex, because their attitude was that sex was like food. When you get hungry, you eat. When your body craves sex, you do the same thing with your sex drive that you do with your hunger. You satisfy it. But in verse 13 Paul says that they were only half right: "Food is for the stomach, and the stomach is for food; but God will do away with both of them. Yet the body is not for immorality, but for the Lord; and the Lord is for the body."

The Corinthians were right about the food part, because the stomach was created for food. In other words, when you get hungry it is OK to eat because God has designed a compartment to receive the food. There's no great issue involved, because someday both food and your stomach will be obsolete. But sex cannot be equated with food—there is much more at stake. God did not put us on earth so that we could indulge our sexual urges. We are to use our bodies—that is, our lives—to glorify Him.

So the question is not whether we have a sexual appetite. The question is, What vehicle has God given us through which to satisfy that appetite? God's only legitimate vehicle for sexual expression is marriage. Unless you start with this mentality, you are going to believe and act on the lie that you can't help yourself. You are going to buy into the line that "this is just the way God made me." Those believers in Corinth were part of a pagan Greek world that taught a two-tiered view of the universe. The Greeks believed that the spiritual and the physical were on two completely separate levels. Therefore you could do what you wanted with your body and not affect your spirit.

God says no to that view. The body and the spirit are closely linked. For the Christian, sex is a spiritual issue. You cannot worship God on Sunday and enter into sexual immorality on Monday and keep those separate, because your body, and not just your spirit, is for the Lord.

In verse 14, Paul refers to God's resurrection power. Remember, he's talking about the body here. What part of us will be raised from the dead someday? Not our spirits, which never die, but our bodies. What Paul is showing is that our bodies have significance beyond the grave, so what we do with our bodies has significance beyond the grave.

I think there's also a question implied here: Do you mean to tell me that God can raise our bodies from the dead but can't help us control our bodies here on earth? That is the question to you and me today. Do we really believe that God's power is so great that He will transform our dead bodies someday, yet His power is not great enough to help us control our sexual appetites today? Anyone who believes that does not understand the resurrection power of Jesus Christ. You do not have to be owned by your passions.

The resurrection of Christ is proof that we have power to control the passions of our bodies until such time as God provides an outlet for them in marriage.

In the church I pastor in Dallas we have a young man who was sexually active before his salvation. But he came, committed his life to Jesus Christ, and became very active in the church. For five years he did not have one sexual encounter. Now God has given him a lovely, godly wife with whom he is free to express his love.

Paul continues his instruction in 1 Corinthians 6:15–17:

> Do you not know that your bodies are members of Christ? Shall I then take away the members of Christ and make them members of a harlot? May it never be! Or do you not know that the one who joins himself to a harlot is one body with her? For He says, "The two will become one flesh." But the one who joins himself to the Lord is one spirit with Him.

Paul has just said that our bodies are for the Lord. Now he elaborates on that truth and gives a practical example of what that means in the area of our sexuality. Because our bodies are members of Christ, when we join our bodies sexually to a harlot (for the Corinthians, the prostitutes in the temple of Aphrodite), we are taking Christ with us.

Someone might say, "I did not invite Christ." Yes, you did—if you belong to Him. You said to Jesus Christ, "Let's You and me go have some fun." See, it is understanding the theology of this issue that begins to make you see that sex is a special area.

Another member of our church is a forty-year-old woman who is a virgin. If you ask her why, she will say, "Because this is not my body. It belongs to Christ. And since it is not my body, no matter what my passions say, I can only do with it what the Owner tells me I can do with it." She once told me, "If I die a virgin, if I have to go to heaven never knowing what it is like to be with a man, it will be worth it to hear Jesus say, `Well done, good and faithful servant.'"

Some people will say this woman is out of her mind. No, she just has a whole different mind. Christianity is a different way of thinking. It is not feeling good about a song the choir sings on Sunday. It is about challenging and controlling the very passions of your life.

Verses 15–17 tell us there is no biblical view of sex without commitment. The only lawful use of sex is within marriage, where two become one. You don't have sex in order to have commitment. You make a commitment first, and then celebrate it with sex. You don't say, "Let's try it, and then I will see whether I want to marry you."

No. You marry me, and then you try it. Women, don't get duped by smooth-talking guys who want to show you love without committing to the love they want to show you. Why? Because you are more valuable than that. You are too valuable to be a toy of undisciplined men who only want to gratify their libidos.

Instead, you hold your head up high and, as Lois did with me, you declare your value. You ask, "Are you willing to put your life on the line for me?" Buying you dinner and a movie is the cheap way out. But when you talk about a lifetime commitment, you will thin out that selfish crowd quickly.

Paul is not saying that sex outside of marriage is wrong simply because two warm bodies come together. Something much more significant is happening. Sex outside of marriage is the ultimate lie, because two people are performing the act of marriage without commitment. No such thing was ever intended in God's economy. Sex without commitment is like chewing a good, juicy steak without swallowing.

Many people, even believers, who have been married for a long time are still suffering from the scars of things that took place perhaps in their teenage years. The reason is that there is no other sin quite like sexual sin, because every other sin is external in its effect. But immorality does damage to the spirit.

Why? Because, as we have seen, Paul says that when you engage in physical intimacy, engagement produces a new thing. The two people become one. There is no other realm, other than when you are joined to Christ in salvation, where this kind of intimacy happens. It is like taking sodium and matching it with chloride. You wind up with salt, which is something brand new. In the same way, when you mix two parts hydrogen with one part oxygen, you get water. When you bring two people together through the sex relationship, the Bible says, you wind up with something brand new.

Now if you decide that you don't want the new thing you just created, if it was just a momentary passion or a fling, then you must pull away. But in the pulling away, you tear away a part of yourself. Obviously, the more times you engage in this destructive process, the more of you is left behind and the greater the damage.

Anyone who has kids knows what it's like to try to get chewing gum out of the carpet, especially after someone has stepped on it. It's a traumatic experience trying to pull that gum out without leaving any behind. Something almost mystical has happened. The merger of the gum with the fiber in the carpet has so integrated them that to get out all the gum, you have to tear away some of the carpet too. And you usually leave some of the gum behind anyway. You may get a lot of it out, but there is always that residue.

So it is when there is a merger of two people in sexual intercourse. When they try to tear that relationship apart, they tear themselves, and a part of them is left behind.

## GUARDING YOUR SEXUAL PURITY

You say, "Tony, this is tough. I want to maintain my purity, but sex is all around me. What do I do?" Paul has a two-word answer for you in verse 18: "Flee immorality." In other words, run! Get out of there. Move your feet. As someone has said, where temptation is present, don't you be present.

You can't emotionalize, theorize, or play with sexual temptation. You have to hit the track and get out of there. You cannot keep placing yourself in environments that are sexually tempting to you and expect to stay clean. That may mean changing your viewing and reading habits, your dating habits, even your friends.

I've done enough traveling to know that when a woman gets on your hotel elevator and wants to know what floor you're staying on, she's not just making conversation. That happened to me once when two young women got on an elevator with me and inquired about my room number. I got off on the next floor because you have to run.

One of the most successful singles in history was a very handsome, sharp young man probably in his midthirties, still a virgin and committed to God. His name was Joseph. Look at Genesis 39:5: "And it came about that from the time [Potiphar] made him overseer in his house, and over all that he owned, the Lord blessed the Egyptian's house on account of Joseph; thus the Lord's blessing was upon all that he owned, in the house and in the field."

Let me tell you something about Joe. He was from a dysfunctional family. His brothers were murderers, thieves, adulterers, and connivers who sold Joseph into slavery. His father, Jacob, was a polygamist. Joseph was from a troubled family, but he turned out fine. As we will see, he held to his purity at all costs.

Does this mean you can have a messed-up family and still turn out fine? Yes, it does. Does this mean you can recover from abuse and live a pure life before God? Yes, it does. You may not have had any control over what happened to you, but part of dealing with it today is understanding that if God is in your life, He can help you make a fresh start.

Verse 6 tells us that "Joseph was handsome in form and appearance." Someone might say that if Joseph is this clean sexually, he has got to be a nerd. No, the brother was cool. The brother was bad. He was a Billy Dee kind of dude. He looked good. He caught your eye. He was well-built. He had it all.

Besides this, Joseph now had some money in his pocket because he had a good job. And he had power because he was over all the house of Potiphar, an important Egyptian official. He was everything any man would want to be.

But Joseph never let the external control the internal. He never let how other people viewed him control what he knew about himself. Joseph belonged to God. He was God's man, and, as a result, he was able to handle what happened next in verses 7–9:

> And it came about after these events that his master's wife looked with desire at Joseph, and she said, "Lie with me." But he refused and said to his master's wife, "Behold, with me here, my master does not concern himself with anything in the house, and he has put all that he owns in my charge. There is no one greater in this house than I, and he has withheld nothing from me except you, because you are his wife. How then could I do this great evil, and sin against God?"

This is powerful stuff. Joseph did not let somebody else's passions control his decisions. Now, this was one needy woman. I take it that Potiphar was always gone because he left everything in Joseph's care. Joseph was always there. She was saying, "I'm being neglected, and I have a problem." But Joseph was saying, "I'm not your solution, lady."

What a beautiful contrast to men who prey on women they know are vulnerable. They find women who may be single, who they know are alone and feeling lonely, and who are probably struggling with sexual temptation, and these men present themselves as the answer to a woman's every need.

---

*With God there is a payday.*

---

Joseph did not let Potiphar's wife control his actions, because his body belonged to God. Notice the focus of Joseph's concern at the end of verse 9. Sexual sin, like all sin, is ultimately against God. Joseph had never read 1 Corinthians 6, but he knew the principle that his body was not his own.

Now I wish I could tell you that once you take this kind of stand, the temptation will go away. We know better than that from Joseph's story. Mrs. Potiphar kept after him "day after day" (v. 10) until she decided to take action.

You probably know what happened. She grabbed him one day and said, "Lie with me!" (v. 12). What did he do? He fled. He left his garment and hit the road. My man lost his shirt over this deal. He left his shirt in her hand and fled the house. As a friend of mine says, "Take the bus, Gus, change the plan, Stan, and give back the key, Lee."

Now please notice. Joseph did not say, "Let me counsel you," or, "Let's talk about it." He got out of there. He ran. It cost him dearly to take a stand, because the woman cried rape, Potiphar believed her, and Joseph wound up in pinstripes (v. 20).

Listen to me. If you decide to guard your sexual purity at all costs, you are going to pay a cost. If you are a man, when some folks find out you are taking your stand, they are going to put you down. They are going to call you a sissy, question your manhood. If you are a woman, some people will think you're an uptight prude. Your friends may accuse you of being too scared to have fun. Some men may try to test your commitment.

If you commit yourself to sexual purity, you may feel as if you're all alone in a mental prison. There is a cost to pay, but with God there is also a payday! Read on in Genesis, and you'll see how God honored and blessed Joseph by elevating him to a high government position in Egypt. God gave him a wife and two sons— and even brought his brothers back and changed them so that they got right.

It may cost you to be faithful to God, but when God rewards you, it will be worth the cost. So I say again, "Flee immorality."

## THE DESTRUCTIVE
## NATURE OF IMMORALITY

Go back to 1 Corinthians 6 and look at the rest of verse 18: "Every other sin that a man commits is outside the body, but the immoral man sins against his own body." There it is. When you develop a lifestyle of immorality, it is unlike any other sin in its destructive nature.

Drugs can't compare to sex in its destructiveness. Crime can't compare with it. Nothing can compare with it because sexual sin carries its own built-in, self-deteriorating mechanism. Why? Because of what we said above: Sex uniquely combines the physical and the spiritual.

The act of sex means that a spiritual relationship has taken place. So when it is an illegitimate spiritual relationship and you back out of it, you back out with spiritual as well as physical damage. Many people don't even know that this is what they are battling in their marriages—the holdover from things that happened earlier but have never been dealt with.

Paul continues in verse 19: "Do you not know that your body is a temple of the Holy Spirit who is in you, whom you have from God, and that you are not your own? For you have been bought with a price: therefore glorify God in your body."

Paul says that if you belong to Christ, your body is a church. Would anybody think about having illicit sex in a church sanctuary on Sunday morning? You say, "Of course not. How could you ask such a thing?" Well, the Bible says that every time you have sexual intercourse, you are in church, because the Spirit is living in your body and your body is His temple.

Immorality is like a cat's paw. When lightly stroked, it is soft and pleasurable. But increased pressure brings out the claws of sin that will shred your very life. The immoral person is like a man who robs a bank and gets what he wants for the moment, but then has to pay the price for a lifetime once he is caught. However, the morally pure person is like a depositor in the bank who puts his money away where it is securely held as the interest builds up, so that he can really enjoy it when it is time to draw on his account.

What we are seeing in our world today is the destruction being wrought by men and women who have taken God's idea of sex and contaminated it. God places a great deal of value on virginity. He places a high value on men and women keeping themselves morally pure until marriage.

Young person, since this is not the message your culture is giving you, you in particular are going to have to be counter-culture. You are going to have to go against the crowd, which as I have suggested may mean being laughed at and called things you don't want to be called because you hold to a standard that most of your peers don't buy anymore. But you're not alone, because that's true for all of us who belong to Christ.

Paul did not skip the subject of sexual morality because he couldn't. He lived in a decrepit world full of incest, debauchery, and prostitution. His world was morally contaminated, and here were these Christians at Corinth, and I'm sure in other places, who had all kinds of questions. How do I control myself in a world like this? What should my attitude toward marriage be?

Sounds familiar, doesn't it? What we're facing is nothing new. Divorce was common in the New Testament world. In fact, in Paul's day it was not uncommon for someone to have been married twenty times. A man could get rid of his wife for almost any reason: she couldn't cook, she was getting a little overweight, the wrinkles were starting to come—wrinkles the husband had no doubt caused! Nevertheless, all these ridiculous things became grounds for divorce. Paul stepped into this madness to tell Christians they had to go against the culture. As we saw earlier, he argued that God created sexuality and therefore He must define it. Any definition of sexuality that leaves God out is a defective definition of the term—and a destructive one.

So the immoral person sins against his own body. That is, when we engage in immorality, we start to self-destruct. There is no area of life that can bring such internal damage, Paul says, as this one.

So it is a very serious thing to unleash one's sexuality outside the safety of a lifelong, one-flesh marriage.

Marriage is God's only word for safe sex. His word is abstinence outside marriage.

You say, "But it's my body."

Not anymore. As we saw in 1 Corinthians 6:19, it is not your body anymore. It is God's house now. You are joined with Christ. So whenever you join yourself to someone else in an illicit relationship, you are using something that doesn't belong to you.

## A CHRISTIAN VIEW OF SEX

Paul has a word for single people and for married couples as he transitions in chapter 7 to answering the questions the Corinthians had written to him. He gets right to the heart of the matter in verse 1: "It is good for a man not to touch a woman." That word *touch* means to light a fire, which came to be understood as a euphemism for sexual passion and activity. Paul says that it is good if that fire is not lit because, once it's lit, it is very hard to extinguish. And, once it's lit, that fire can easily burn out of control.

Since Paul says that it is good not to light the fire of sexual passion, the Bible's word to singles is that your singleness can never be good unless it is celibate. Now we know that Paul is about to go on and tell us there is a proper place for the fire, so if you're single now that doesn't mean you will never get married and know legitimate sexual expression. But as long as you are single, you will never understand God's intent for your singleness until you are celibate.

If you are single and acting as if you're married—

that is, if you are unmarried but are physically involved with another person so that you are functioning as married people—that is not good. Your singleness will never be good under God until it is a celibate singleness. If you are trying to live in two worlds at one time, you will never know the good and God-honoring single life Paul talks about. In fact, Paul is so high on singleness that he says, "I wish that all men were [unmarried] even as I myself am" (v. 7).

Single person, if you really want to maximize your singleness, it is good to avoid lighting the fire of sexual passion, to abstain from immorality. Then God will bless and maximize your singleness, and you will find the fulfillment and meaning and direction He wants you to have.

Why is it good not to touch a woman? Because in Corinth it was considered good to touch a woman—any woman—anytime you felt like it, under any circumstances. The whole philosophy was that this was your thing. Do what you want to do. Immorality was considered just a normal thing, something good to do. Paul says this is not good because God says it is not good.

So to avoid "immoralities" (v. 2; the plural refers to various kinds of immorality, whether homosexuality or incest or whatever) and to give a proper outlet for the expression of our God-given sexual drive, Paul reminds the Corinthians that God has given us marriage. But not just any old kind of marriage or any number of marriages. God's ideal is still one man and one woman for life.

Marriage is God's context where immorality does not exist. Hebrews 13:4 says that marriage is honorable and that God will judge those who practice sex outside of His honorable standards.

As I said, Paul defines marriage as one man and one woman. God made Adam and Eve, not Adam and Steve. There is no provision in God's Word for homosexual relationships that are called marriages. Paul also strikes a blow against polygamy, which was never God's intention, although He permitted it for a period of time.

So Paul says that to avoid immorality, what men and women must do is save themselves for marriage. The fact is that some people were so sexually active before they got married that they were running on low octane after they got married. Their passions burned too early, and now they had burned low because they did not keep what was special and sacred for the marriage bed.

God wants all your passions reserved. You say, "But they are building up." Good. Let them increase and build. Pack them up so that when God does call you into a marriage relationship, you can operate on high octane, super-unleaded and not just on regular.

Young woman, don't let any smooth-talking guy tell you that because he washed his car, got his hair cut, got all shined up, took you out, and spent all this money on you, he's done his job. Now it's time for you to do yours. Tell him to forget it. He can't make sexual demands on you just because he washed his car, pressed his clothes, got a haircut, and spent money taking you out. He can take his money and go home. If necessary, offer to help him put the dirt back on his car, rewrinkle his clothes, and let his hair grow back. Then tell him good-bye.

Why? Because you are not for sale. Remember, after the intimacy, when he walks away, he takes part of you with him. Outside of marriage, you have no sexual obligation just because a guy is nice. Until he is willing to give all of himself to you, he can demand nothing from you. If he says, "If you loved me, you would," you say, "Then I guess I don't love you, because I won't!"

God's idea is that the sexual relationship is to be preserved for one man and one woman in the context of marriage. Sex is not a way to say thanks for a nice evening. Sex was not given for you to release tension. There are a lot of other things, from organized sports to exercise, that can do that. Sex was not given so that you can feel good. It was given to express your total commitment to another person.

So you wait until God gives you that person. You pray for that person. Then, when God grants you that person, you express your commitment in the intimacy of that relationship.

## SEXUAL INTIMACY WITHIN MARRIAGE

Paul was not a prudish, self-righteous single person who looked down on those who could not control their passions. It is possible that Paul was married at one time, because he had been a member of the Sanhedrin, the Jewish ruling council, whose members were required to be married.

Whether Paul was an exception to the rule, a widower, or whatever, we don't know. We do know that he speaks forthrightly about the subject of the intimacy of marriage and does not apologize for it.

Look at verse 3 of 1 Corinthians 7: "Let the husband fulfill his duty to his wife, and likewise also the wife to her husband." This word duty can cause great consternation. Is marital intimacy supposed to be a job? Many times it can feel like it.

What does Paul mean? I believe he is talking about the distinction between physical intimacy between Christian couples and physical intimacy between non-Christian couples. You may need to think about that one for a minute. You may say, "Wait a minute, Tony. I thought it was all the same thing." No, physical intimacy between non-Christians is primarily self-generated— this is what I want. Physical intimacy among Christians is designed to be other-generated—this is what my mate needs.

Now, I am not saying that every single unbeliever in every single case is self-motivated. And I would not try to claim that every Christian marriage reflects the ideal of selfless giving. I'm talking about an overall pattern.

By the way, Paul's order in verse 3 is important. It's the husband's responsibility to take the lead, and his wife's calling is to respond.

Many men have said to me, "I would love to fulfill my duty to my wife, but she won't let me." That could be because what you are offering to fulfill, she does not need. One of the great challenges in building true physical intimacy is understanding what the other person needs.

What a woman needs starts in the morning and not at night. What a woman needs starts in the kitchen and not in the bedroom. What a woman needs starts with her emotions and not with her body. When some husbands say they want to meet their wives' needs, they are talking about something far different from what their wives understand by that phrase.

---

*This revelation will shock many husbands.*

---

If a husband is really serious about meeting his wife's needs, he will talk with her more, he will compliment her more. He will still be dating her and embracing her when he has nothing else on his mind but an expression of affection. Listen to me, husband. If the only time your wife knows she has your undivided attention is at 10:00 P.M., when you want to be intimate, if she knows that the only time you are going to compliment, recognize, esteem, and value her is at 10:00 P.M., then, because you have not met her emotional needs, which began at 10:00 A.M., you are not fulfilling your duty to your mate.

That is why 1 Peter 3:7 tells us husbands to understand our wives. Most of our wives were attracted to us at least in part because of what we did during the dating period. One thing we were able to do was rap. I must admit that I was among the best. We men get off on our ability to compliment a woman and be smooth with our words. That was important when we were dating.

Another thing a lot of men were good at when they were dating their future wives was making them feel special, planning little surprises. They would open the car door and wait until the lady got in, then close it softly behind her. Now she is lucky to get in before hubby drives off. When she was about to go through a door, the guy would open it for her. Now the door hits her as he walks through ahead of her.

See, husband, what made your wife want to marry you was not your jumping up and talking about your physical attributes. It was the fact that you met a need in her. When that need is met in marriage, physical intimacy is not a problem. In other words, a husband is not fulfilling his duty to his wife unless he is providing what she needs.

This will be a shocking revelation to many husbands, but I'll risk it anyway: one of the best ways to find out what your wife needs is to ask. To assume that what you are offering is what the other person needs is the height of arrogance. Wives tell us they need affection and a sense of security, communication, and a sense of being cared for and esteemed.

That is why, when the romance leaves a marriage,

the wife's passion for sex dies. Not so with men. Men don't have to have all that relationship stuff. It's nice, but it is extra. You can make a man mad at 10:00 P.M., and at 10:05 he is fine. You make a woman mad at 10:00 A.M., and, if that thing is not fixed, she is not fine at 10:00 P.M. In fact, she may not be fine at 10:00 P.M. for a month.

I'm not saying it's good that men are like this. I'm saying that's the way it is. We men have a long way to go in learning the art of intimacy with our wives. We need to learn that for our wives intimacy involves the whole person and the whole house. It involves the compliment you make about the meal, how you come in the door when you come home from work, and how you treat her when she comes home from work, if that's the case.

When couples come in to see me and say they have a physical problem, that is rarely true. In most cases what they have is an intimacy problem, a relational problem. Because of this, they cannot get the physical part of their marriage on track. But the physical is not the problem. In fact, I would say that married couples who have a good relationship but know little about sexual intimacy can have better intimacy than a couple who know all about the technical aspects of sex but have a poor relationship.

The fundamental issue is expressed in that word *duty*. Husband, your duty is to your wife, not to you. When many men say, "I want to meet her needs," what they really mean is, "I want her to meet my needs."

That is not what Paul says. He says that the issue for the husband is his wife's needs. Until a husband is willing to take the time and make the investment in order to understand his wife and her needs, he will never be able to meet them.

Now, Paul knows this is a two-way street. The second half of verse 3 is as important as the first half. If a husband is meeting his wife's needs, her duty is to reciprocate, to respond.

In other words, wife, your husband cannot date you and care for you and compliment you and serve you, and make sure your needs are met, only to have you deny his needs. You cannot be on the receiving end and not on the giving end. You cannot receive his love and affection and not meet your duty to him.

Look at verse 4: "The wife does not have authority over her own body, but the husband does; and likewise also the husband does not have authority over his own body, but the wife does." When a husband is fulfilling his duty to his wife, the wife responds and meets her responsibility to her husband by coming under his authority or control. This is what the word *authority* means.

The wife relinquishes control of her body to the touch, the care, the caress, the love of her husband. Then, as the husband responds to his wife's response, he also relinquishes control of his body. The picture here is of two people who are learning that they belong totally to each other. In some mysterious way, when two people are intimate there is a giving of themselves, a vulnerability, a yielding of control. Sex should be the ultimate act of self-giving rather than a selfish act done to fulfill one's own needs.

By now you may be thinking that we have left the subject of sexual purity and are talking about marriage. That's understandable because, to most of us, sexual purity means we're going to talk about premarital sex and how to keep yourself pure until marriage and avoid temptation and all those issues. Well, we've dealt with these, but the Bible's picture of sexual purity takes in the whole range of our sexuality, including marriage. What I'm saying is that the stuff we are talking about here is as important a part of the subject of sex as all the premarital and extramarital issues.

If you have read the Bible much, you know that the Song of Solomon contains the Bible's most unblushing description of sexual intimacy in marriage. Chapter 4 describes the buildup to intimacy in great detail, and the beauty of it is that you see the self-giving between Solomon and his wife, the mutual yielding of their bodies. Notice that the intimacy begins with Solomon's compliments and words of admiration and appreciation for his bride, not with the physical act of sex. But when the moment of intimacy occurs, God Himself invites the lovers to enjoy one another (see 5:1).

When this kind of intimacy occurs within marriage, God blesses it. When it occurs outside marriage, God condemns it. God so believes in this kind of marital intimacy that He recorded it, detail for detail, in the Bible.

It is a matter of control. You give up control of your body when you fulfill your duty to your mate, which means meeting his or her needs first and not yours. Then, when your mate has met his or her duty, you give up authority to that person. You say, "I am relinquishing control over my body because you have fulfilled your duty to meet my needs."

When I delivered this message, I asked the men in my church some practical questions. When was the last time you dated your wife? When was the last time you surprised her? When was the last time you caressed her in a nonsexual way, or noticed the new dress or the new hairdo? When was the last time you picked up the phone and simply said, "I just called to say hello. I am in a hurry, but I just can't get my mind off of you"?

See, husband, when you meet your wife's needs, then she responds by welcoming you, by letting you know that she is willing to give up authority over her body to you. There is nothing that can overpower this kind of intimacy. This is how God wants it.

Before we wrap this up with some application and a discussion of what to do if you've already blown it sexually, I want to consider 1 Corinthians 7:5. We have said that outside marriage there is to be no sexual intimacy. But Paul makes clear in this verse that within marriage sexual intimacy is to be the norm. Just as single people aren't to act married, married people are not to act single.

"Stop depriving one another," Paul says. The reference is to sexual intimacy. He says this to prevent either partner in a marriage from putting the other partner in a situation that will make that person vulnerable to immorality (see 1 Thessalonians 4:3–7, an important passage that lays out the principle of sexual faithfulness and purity for marrieds and singles).

If you are single, the way you avoid immorality is by not putting yourself in compromising situations. Paul has already addressed this in verse 1, as we saw. So we talked about ways to protect yourself as a single person.

One of the ways you protect yourself from falling into immorality as a married person is that you do not deprive your mate of sexual intimacy, with one exception, which Paul spells out clearly in verse 5. Other than uncontrollable things such as illness, there is only one situation in which sexual intimacy is not to be regular in a marriage: an agreed-upon period of focused prayer.

First, I want to underline the agreement part of this. This is not a unilateral decision that one partner is going to take six months off. Paul says it must be by mutual agreement. Second, the time is to be limited. After you have devoted yourselves to prayer, you resume normal sexual relations so that Satan doesn't tempt you because of your lack of self-control.

For want of a better label, I call this "sexual fasting." Stay with me on this for a minute, because the Bible has something important to teach married couples here about a different kind of intimacy that can be as satisfying as sexual intimacy.

Fasting is giving up a craving of the body because of a greater need of the spirit. Most of us relate fasting only to food, a period during which you give up food and spend the time you would normally be eating in prayer because of a deep spiritual need in your life.

---

*Nothing will bring a couple closer than praying together.*

---

In fact, Jesus said that some things come about only by fasting and prayer. So if you have a need in your life and you have never fasted over it, you have not fully addressed it yet. Fasting is one of the lost arts of spiritual discipline today.

For instance, if you have a child who has gone astray and who is a deep spiritual burden, have you fasted over the problem yet? Recently some people in our church gave incredible testimonies of how God supernaturally entered in and met a need when they fasted and prayed.

What Paul is talking about here is a time when there is a deep spiritual need in your life as a married couple, and in order to get that need met you give up a craving of the body. In this case, the physical appetite you give up is not your hunger for food but your craving for sexual intimacy with your mate. The two of you take the time that you would normally spend being physically intimate to be spiritually intimate with each other and God.

We know from passages like Exodus 19:9–15 that, when God was getting ready to meet with the children of Israel, one of the ways He commanded them to prepare themselves for this meeting was by abstaining from any sexual contact. In other words, there was to be total concentration, total focus on this spiritual invasion of God. So Paul is on solid biblical ground when he says that a sexual fast is legitimate for a married couple.

One of the great things a husband and wife can do is to set aside sex for a sexual fast so that they can pray together, rather than a sexual deprivation that is based on anger or headaches or any of that. Imagine the intimacy a couple will experience when they kneel together to plead with God to intervene in a situation. Imagine a husband taking the spiritual lead to propose a sexual fast to his wife for the purpose of concentrated prayer together. That alone would totally revolutionize many Christian marriages!

Nothing will bring a husband and wife closer together than praying together. If you want to increase your intimacy with each other, then take that time and give it to prayer, and you will be amazed at how God changes your spirit and your attitude. If you need an invasion from God in your affairs as a couple or as a family, He calls on you to set aside time and sacrifice physical intimacy for spiritual intimacy with Him.

In Joel 2:12–16, the Lord Himself calls for the people to fast in repentance for their sins, and He says, "Let the bridegroom come out of his room and the bride out of her bridal chamber" (v. 16). In other words, let married couples cease their sexual activity in order to fast and pray for the Lord's mercy and forgiveness. Whatever need or burden a married couple may be facing, it is appropriate for them to abstain from sex by agreement for a time of prayer.

But that is the only time there is not to be regular intimacy in a marriage. Paul then closes this section of teaching with several statements on the benefits of singleness. The admonition in verse 9 reminds us of what we talked about earlier. The only good form of singleness is celibacy, not a sexually active singleness that lights the fires of passion.

So the word for singles is abstinence, which God has the power to enable any single person to achieve for His glory. The word for married people is sexual faithfulness and exclusivity for life with each other.

### WHERE TO GO FROM HERE

We've presented a lot of material and a lot of ideas. Let me try to extract some principles from what we've talked about and give you some ideas you can use to help guard your sexual purity regardless of your marital status. Then I want to say something to you if your need is forgiveness and restoration.

First of all, make a covenant with your eyes (Job 31:1). The patriarch Job said he would not allow himself to give in to the lust of his eyes when it came to other women. That's a great place to start. Watch what you watch so that what you watch does not start watching you back.

Second, we learned a practical truth concerning sexual temptation in 1 Corinthians 6:18. Run. Get out of there. If you have to, start running now.

Third, if you are married, Proverbs 5:15–19 says that you need to look for and find your sexual fulfillment at home. Put forth the effort to build intimacy with your mate, and the result will be more than satisfying. God will reward your commitment with satisfaction you never imagined possible.

Fourth, Colossians 3:5 says to resist the flesh because our flesh is being pulled at all day. You need to watch the environments you place yourself in. You need to examine your spirit to make sure that you are not putting yourself in compromising situations and settings, knowingly or unknowingly.

In cities such as Dallas there are plenty of "gentleman's" clubs that serve as counterfeit churches, where people go for fellowship and to bring themselves under the control of someone else—except that, in this case, the fellowship is built around lust, and the controlling agent is alcohol, not the Holy Spirit. It's obvious that this is not the proper environment for someone who has made a covenant with his eyes, seeks to guard his spirit, and resists the pull of the flesh.

Fifth, if you have been sexually abused, you can, by the grace of God, forgive your abuser so that you can put the past behind you and enjoy your present and future. While you still bear the stain of the abuse, you are going to have to forgive the abuser and place him or her in the hands of God so that you can move on with your life.

Sixth, Romans 12:1 says to present your body a living sacrifice to God. Present yourself fully to God. Get busy for the kingdom. When Adam was single, he was busy naming the animals. God gave Adam something significant to do before He gave him Eve.

Men, don't go around thinking, *Where is Eve?* Women, don't go around looking for Adam. Go around doing the work of God's kingdom, and He will take you to your Adam or Eve when it is time for you to meet them. Don't worry. If God has prepared a man or woman for you, someone else is not going to slip in and marry that person. God is capable of keeping your Adam or Eve for you.

Seventh, if you are single, reclaim the glory of your virginity. You can never become a physical virgin again once you have surrendered that, but you can get the glory of your virginity back again. By this I mean you can determine that from this point on you are going to carry and conduct yourself as one who has never been touched and who has that commitment to present to a future mate.

If you are married, this means you will carry and conduct yourself as a faithful one-woman or one-man person so that the stains of any failure you have had will be overcome by your renewed commitment to your marriage.

## A WORD ABOUT FORGIVENESS

Talking about recapturing the glory of purity makes this a good place for a final word about forgiveness and restoration. Actually, the word I have for you is not mine but Jesus' word.

There is no greater example of Jesus' attitude toward a repentant sexual sinner than his encounter with the woman caught in adultery (John 8:1–11). If you're familiar with the story, you know that the whole scene came about because the Jews were always trying to trick Jesus.

So they brought this woman to Him, knowing that the Law declared she should be stoned to death. They made it a point to explain to Jesus that she had been caught in the very act. "We caught her committing adultery. What do you say, Jesus?"

Since this was a public scene, we can imagine this woman's sense of humiliation as she stood before the sinless Son of God. Sexual sin always brings a painful sense of humiliation and shame, because something that was designed to be intimate and private has been given away. If you have committed sexual sin, you probably know how this woman felt.

Jesus responded to their accusation and demand by bending down and writing in the sand. Two thousand years' worth of Bible commentators have tried to figure out what Jesus wrote, but, whatever it was, He stood up and hit the scribes and Pharisees with a heavy one: "He who is without sin among you, let him be the first to throw a stone at her" (v. 7).

Then He started writing on the ground again as these self-righteous but equally guilty sinners melted away one by one into the crowd. When Jesus stood up the second time, no one was left but the woman and Him.

I think what Jesus wrote in the sand had to do with the correct reading of the Law on adultery, because the scene before Him was all messed up. The woman's accusers were only half right. If she was indeed caught in the act of adultery, this woman was deserving of the death penalty under the Mosaic Law. But the law also stipulated that the man die.

However, these men did not bring the guilty man, even though they knew who this man was, since they caught them in "the very act." This showed that they weren't really interested in justice or God's honor or any of the stuff that mattered. If they were, there would have been two guilty people standing before Jesus, not one. They were just using this woman and exploiting her shame to do their own dirty work.

So Jesus wrote once, then twice. He was saying that if we are going to condemn this woman by the Law, then let's get the Law straight. Two people have to die here, not one.

Then there was another thing. The stone thrower could not be guilty of the same crime as the accused. You could not pick up a stone and kill somebody else for committing adultery if you too had committed adultery, because then you would have to undergo the same sentence after they finished with the other person.

What I mean is that Jesus' statement about throwing the first stone is more specific than we usually understand it to be. This is usually interpreted to mean that Jesus was saying that a person had to be perfect before he could throw a stone at someone else.

But if that were the case, the Law would never have been carried out even in the Old Testament economy, because there are no perfect people. Jesus is not talking about being perfect. He is saying that the only ones qualified to stone this woman were the ones who were not guilty of the same sin. That thinned the crowd out really quick. The men left one by one because Jesus could then condemn them to the same penalty of stoning if they were to cast a stone at the woman, since they had done the same thing themselves—perhaps with this same woman.

But the best part is what Jesus said to the woman. He saw into her heart and said, "Neither do I condemn you; go your way. From now on sin no more" (v. 11). That's the word of forgiveness I leave with you if you will come clean about your sexual sin.

You must bring it to Jesus with a repentant heart and confess it. If you will do that, He will forgive you, and you can go on your way restored, with His power available to keep you from falling into sexual sin again. Notice that Jesus neither minimized this woman's sin nor pummeled her with it, as the others wanted to do. He recognized it, forgave it, and told her to turn from it.

So let me repeat the challenge I made to you to reclaim your sexual purity. Even if you are no longer a physical virgin, you can commit yourself to sexual purity and faithfulness "from now on." This is not to pretend that there is not residual damage from sexual sin. But forgiveness means you can stop the damage now and enjoy the blessing of purity from here on out.

If you are married, I urge you to renew your commitment to your partner. If you are still a virgin, make a vow to God that you will remain pure until He brings somebody into your life. God will be a lot more responsive to your prayers about the future if you are living for Him now. Remember, true decisions are not made; they are lived.

I have tried as honestly as possible to share God's Word with you on this sensitive subject. May God help us in the church to resist the world's attempts to make us be something other than what He wants us to be.

# THE URBAN ALTERNATIVE

## The Philosophy

Dr. Tony Evans and TUA believe the answer to transforming our culture comes from the inside out and from the bottom up. We believe the core cause of the problems we face is a spiritual one; therefore, the only way to address them is spiritually. And that means the proclamation and application of biblical principles to the four areas of life—the individual, the family, the church, and the community. We've tried a political, social, economic, and even a religious agenda. It's time for a kingdom agenda.

## The Purpose

We believe that when each biblical sphere of life functions properly, the net result is evangelism, discipleship, and community impact. As people learn how to govern themselves under God, they then transform the institutions of family, church, and government from a biblically based kingdom perspective.

## The Programs

To achieve our goal we use a variety of strategies, methods, and resources for reaching and equipping as many people as possible.

- Broadcast Media
  The Urban Alternative reaches hundreds of thousands of people each day with a kingdom-based approach to life through its daily radio program, weekly television broadcast, and the Internet.

- Leadership Training
  Our national Church Development Conference, held annually, equips pastors and lay leaders to become agents of change. Teaching biblical methods of church ministry has helped congregations renew their sense of mission and expand their ministry impact.

- Crusades/Conferences
  Crusades are designed to bring churches together across racial, cultural, and denominational lines to win the lost. TUA also seeks to keep these churches together for ongoing fellowship and community impact. Conferences give Christians practical biblical insight on how to live victoriously in accordance with God's Word and His kingdom agenda in the four areas of life—personal, family, church, and community.

- Resource Development
  We are fostering lifelong learning partnerships with the people we serve by providing a variety of published materials. We offer books, audiotapes,

videos, and booklets to strengthen people in their walk with God and ministry to others.

- Project Turn-Around
  PTA is a comprehensive church-based community impact strategy. It addresses such areas as economic development, education, housing, health revitalization, family renewal and reconciliation. To model the success of the project, TUA invests in its own program locally. We also assist other churches in tailoring the model to meet the specific needs of their communities, while simultaneously addressing the spiritual and moral frame of reference.

* * *

For more information, a catalog of Dr. Tony Evans's ministry resources, and a complimentary copy of Dr. Evans's monthly devotional magazine,

call (800) 800-3222 or

write TUA at P.O. Box 4000, Dallas TX 75208.